TAPESTRY
of LOVE AND LOSS

By Patrick Wood

BROWN COUNTY PUBLISHING

Copyright © 2012 by Patrick Wood

ISBN-10: 0615639232
EAN-13: 978-0615639239
Library of Congress Control Number: 2012939176
CreateSpace, North Charleston, South Carolina
Title ID 3866256
Printed in the United States of America
Cover Designs by Anne Wood

First Edition

DEDICATION

To the sweetest buds of all the roses
where beauty blooms within and without

Sweet Marsey
Maggs, Annie and Kate

CONTENTS

TAPESTRY
of LOVE AND LOSS

Introduction

When I was in my youth, I started writing poetry and short stories as I traveled the world. Having adventures in Peru, Ireland, Spain, Morocco and other places as well as the United States, those times and events have long passed but the memories lived on in my writings.

Last year, I began to reread a number of pieces developed from those earlier years and realized that after much culling, there were a few gems among the shards of glass worth sharing.

Some of my compositions are about love such as "In the Wake of Love" and "When". Others are about loss such as "Altered" and "Divergence". The rest of this work lies somewhere between the cracks of both love and loss. Inherent within some of these verses is the influence of Burns, Yeats, Dickinson, Housman and other poets. I thank them for their gifts and apologize for making their association with my work.

Step out and embrace the passing of things, the unceasing movement of time and all the excitement it has to offer. May some of this poetry inspire you as you create your own adventures along the highways and byways of life.

ALTERED

Everyone's got planes to catch, schedules to keep
Death is the great disrupter

The news "the eagle has flown" shatters forever an
    everyday gait and harmony—

A grayish tint usurps all the colors of the sky
Every note of song falls flat upon the ear
A blanket of cold is dumped that chills to the bone
Then the sadness sets in…

Warriors carrying a block of wood to bury harshly
    in the ground
Remnants of tear streaks scar the face; elongated
    stamps seen by all who look
Faint memories of warmth linger on in tandem
    with a smoldering sorrow

Residuals of hope left in those who wait

END OF DAY

It's cold outside and the wind starts to blast
And I am getting older as you well know
If I could hold you for awhile in my arms
I would never let go, never let go

The halls are dark and the candles snuffed out
The fires burned down and the wood all gone
If I could warm you with my worn out cloak
You'd feel better 'fore long, better 'fore long

The sunny days have all passed us by
The moon and the stars have played through their
     part
The last tiny refuge where we have to hide
Is a memory of mine, a piece of my heart

MORNING HANGOVER

One night the boat docked in Rosslare
We built a fire on the shore
The boys searched the beach for mussels
Logs burned, we looked for more

We climbed the hill to the local bar
We took our turns singing with the band
She sat in the front row eyeing us
Brave new Americans in a brand new land

Down by the water under the moon
Bodies groping, tussling, a foot
When the dawn's light floated into the cove
Her imprint was left in the soot

Midmorning we found ourselves hitching a ride
Not a car to see our thumbs high
A truck rushed past and she with her man
Didn't even wave good-bye

EMPTY

I gathered a huge pile of gold
I beat them all back and I won
By measures of loot I had made it
Sadly without any fun

I won every competitive game
I broke them and tore them apart
By record of wins I had made it
Sadly without any heart

I amassed more materials than most
I sought and achieved every goal
As a king of luxury I had made it
Sadly without any soul

WHIRLPOOLS

Lives of purpose swept away
Clinging wistfully to past repose
Minds engaged in pragmatic gods
The bloom long off the rose

Webs of silver spun so thin
Fallen, fragile traps of lust
Chaotic, fearful driving torture
Writhing, twisting lines of dust

The monadic peoples swirl around
Grasping, pinching daily bread
Biding time as time bides them
Poof—and then they're dead

IN THE WAKE OF LOVE

When youth was in its vigor
And time had not yet had its way
The sport of love will ravage
Arrows of conquest on display

When Helen left her lover king
And sailed with her new boy
Love's account was left untallied
Mycenae's war with Troy

Now at greater ages
Love—won, lost and in arrears
Fury once enflamed in arrows
Left a wake of tears

DIVERGENCE

A deep sadness lingers on our shoulders
Like a gray mantle of external night
She who was lent to us for such a short time has
    departed
Taking with her our best memories

If only we had not loved so well
These days would be easier to pace
But now we are left alone at a finish line
That came way too soon

Laughter, melody, a soaring poetry of life
Now a limp and tattered coat lying peacefully on
    the bed
Surrounded by deaf mutes she once called her own

Dusk

Riding north across the hills
The empire once began
The hope was with the younger lads
Who followed the older man

Lo, the new day's coming
The lads have promised all
But with their father's fading
Their vows have lost the call

Now the sun has set on fields
And silence spreads so wide
The tired man lies down to sleep
His weary dreams subside

❧

THE RUNNER

All we know is
Time passes…

There is a long run ahead—
A run that will exact the measure of a long distance
    runner

Those we know will want to rest
They will try to spill off
Slip by the roadside

They try in vain to protect themselves: their bodies
I do not
Yet why am I the runner
Why do I have the strength
Why do I have the resilience they so conserved all
    their lives

Why am I the one—
The one left to put the faces back on the wall

WHEN

When the world starts spinning in reverse
When the sun stops shining each new morn
When the stars fall out of the night time skies
When the oceans cover up all the lands–

That's when I'll stop loving you

Memories of Mollendo

Twenty-one years had passed since I had last seen their summer home in the port of Mollendo. It was parked close to the Pacific Ocean and I remember one night listening to the waves bouncing along the shore. We ran down to the beach after the town went to sleep. We lay there in the sand making angel prints under the glimmering stars. The waves beckoned to us like mermaids and we shed our clothing to crash their rhythmic rituals.

Later, back at the house, we downed shots of Pisco and played cards while listening to the sounds of a joyous night. At dawn, that fragile turn of day, we dropped into a deep sleep. Ah, how I was in love with my "morena" from Mollendo.

Twenty-one years had passed since I had last seen their summer home. The walls were cracking and crumbling. The roof was half pulled away. Industrious spiders had webbed ceilings and corners. Rubbish flowed over the tile worn floors. I walked out on the second story terrace and gazed quietly over the town which seemed as if it had always been there, kind of like a floating dream. I thought of her again and of those whom I had known long ago in this place.

They remained behind me like flickering shadows locked up in a beautiful memory...once recalled, but not summoned to follow me as I walked away to the car.

SLIP STRING DIMENSIONS

I walked alone in the graveyard at night
I spied the big cross—the figure in white
I saw the ghosts rising—the heroes, the slime
I slipped down the path again biding my time

I checked back in to the asylum today
I saw my good woman—she started to pray
I watched the gray ashes changing to flowers
I heard muffled voices decay with the hours

I found myself there in the office quicksand
I jerked up the screen, wand in my hand
I'm here in the battle, fighting the cause
I'm a zapper of one; I'm the Wizard of Oz

I'm a proton, an atom, a mutant, a quark
I'm a closer, baggage handler, chameleon, a spark
I'm merging the past with the buzz future thing
I'm traveling the universe pulling a string

I walked alone in the graveyard at night
I spied the big cross—the figure in white
I saw the ghosts rising—the heroes, the slime
I slipped down the path again biding my time

❖ ❖ ❖

Coming of Age

Gone are the days of hopscotch, popsicles, bruises
on the knee, catching frogs and bicycle rides
Gone are the nights of fireflies, Halloween masks,
hide 'n seek and marshmallow campfires
Gone are the times of everyday hugs, bed time
kisses and holding hands on travels to and fro

Yet, every now and then…when the moon turns a
dark colored orange
When the stars congeal at the left corner of the
Milky Way
When an unannounced comet inexplicably races
across the sky—

She appears again—that beautiful soul with
sparkling blue eyes, smoky blond hair and easy
smiles, caught between youth and woman
If only for a brief and shining moment, she's that
sweet Margie from an age passed by

✵ ✵ ✵

FLIGHT OF PRAYER

A man said a prayer in the Cordoba Mosque
A prayer with the wisdom of sages
He prayed as an Arab; he prayed as a Jew
He prayed as a Christian, a prayer for all ages

In varied voices and tongues rose the prayer
A prayer for family and friend
He spoke of his thoughts, of loves and losses
And skirmishes on the mend

Innocence, charity, laughter and faith
Passed from his heart to the others
The Lord heard his prayer in the Cordoba Mosque
And passed it along to his brothers

FAR IN A WINDY NIGHT TIME

There by the starlit stones
A girl draws by and hears
A gentle soul a whispering
"love you" between the tears

She feels the stirring memories
Places where they were known
And here he lies so peacefully
Taking his rest alone

Far in a windy night time
She'll join her lover's rest
They'll be entwined forever
Eternity—as her guest

NOBLE SPORT

To the bull, a matador is strange
He runs at each move for trust is neither born nor
  bred
The music box figure dressed in dainty slippers
  thrusts out at him
Heavy with tradition and history
The bull is masculine, teaming with power
The one with slippers is venerated, even adulated

The grand dancer stalks the toro with precise steps
A ballet across the clay sod floor
Red silk is flashing in the sun glazed coliseum
Lancers on horseback stick with storied pain
Darts stab and cling without quarter
The raging mass charges for the finale
He is staring with head bowed low
The gleam of metal thrusts between the horns
He sways, he whirls, he falls on his knees
The spectator frenzy subsides

His death is the afternoon's entertainment
His epitaph is tonight's feast at the local hotel

FLAMENCO GYPSY

If he were young he would marry
A Flamenco dancer in black
With green eyes jetting fire
Whirling, stamping, snorting

Like a horse bucking free from the corral
She turns flicking and snapping
The guitar hammers and wails
She lifts her head and smiles
Her glance flirts without discrimination
Her scarf waves; her skirt sweeps
She flails the floor with winged feet

He returns to his spent youth
Mesmerized by her and the dance
Her hard shoes forever tap an arrhythmia into his
    heart

MEDITERRANEO HYPNOTICO

An easy tropical beat of the Mediterranean waves
A sheet of white and yellow speckles shining from
    sea up to the sky
The spell is out there for all to obey

Sands humming on the shores
Caressing the shore and vibrating the ambulatory
    souls
A primal urge manifests a shriek of happiness
Waves wash the dunes and hypnotize the lone
    walkers
They flee the aimless world; fugitives from mindless
    toil

The celebrating sea minstrel beckons the fools to
    dance
And dance and dance 'til they drop of exhaustion
Soon dawn lights up the swell of God's creation

YOUR SMILE

Your smile illuminates
Your smile sets my heart aglow
Your smile spreads its wings
In my eyes, in my soul

Your smile conjures many thoughts
Your smile moves an evening breeze
Your smile shakes the star filled heavens
Over the land, over the seas

THE VOICES OF OTTER LAKE

Tales being told at campfires
Each story – a shadowy tone
Winds blowing to unknown places
Hopeful mornings, nights of stone

Spirits lingering into the night
Ghosts now lost to their fate
Recounting the bittersweet times
The memories of Otter Lake

Cattails are starting to whisper
The secrets they used to know
Songs of contemplation
Bred in the lake long ago

Down at the dock the moon dozes
Near the watery inlet I wait
I pause to listen to voices
The voices of Otter Lake

❧

Patrick Wood

ENCHANTMENT

When dusk begins to settle in
And children have gone to sleep
The fairies rise up from the mists
Their promises to keep

They roam the meadows and the wood
To find the friends they had
Beautiful, sweet and pretty lasses
Many a brave and valorous lad

Then the morning sun emerges
The fairies disappear
Gone again for quite some time
Another day, another year

www.ingramcontent.com/pod-product-compliance
Lightning Source LLC
Chambersburg PA
CBHW030011040426
42337CB00012BA/736